Editor
Heather Douglas

Illustrator
Blanca Apodaca

Cover Artists
Denise Bauer
Marilyn Goldberg

Editor in Chief
Ina Massler Levin, M.A.

Creative Director
Karen J. Goldfluss, M.S. Ed.

Art Production Manager
Kevin Barnes

Art Coordinator
Renée Christine Yates

Imaging
James Edward Grace

Publisher
Mary D. Smith, M.S. Ed.

Author

Jessica M. Dubin Kissel, M.A.

Teacher Created Resources, Inc.
6421 Industry Way
Westminster, CA 92683
www.teachercreated.com

ISBN: 978-1-4206-5981-8

© 2008 Teacher Created Resources, Inc.
Made in U.S.A.

Table of Contents

Introduction

As part of students' mathematical journey, they study the skill of Skip Counting. Skip Counting is the process of skipping numbers as counting occurs (e.g. 2, 4, 6…). Skip Counting, also known as Number Patterns, helps students relate to numbers, and count in a faster, more efficient manner. Skip Counting also begins the study of multiplication.

In this book, we have concentrated on skip counting by twos through tens, and from one through fifty. The activities have been developed for the primary grades where concentration and mental dexterity need constant practice.

You will find 59 different number patterns on the following pages that will delight your students. They are designed to challenge your students but not frustrate them. These activities will also enforce language and fine motor skills.

Having students create their own number patterns would reinforce and further their understanding of the subject. As you move through the year, and their skills become more advanced, why not have them create their own worksheets that reflect their newly acquired knowledge? Students can use subject matters of their own personal interests. Or, as a group assignment, your students might enjoy coming up with their own worksheets that will challenge the other groups in the classroom.

We hope that these worksheets provide hours of enjoyment for your class. Have fun!

Hearing Ears

Draw a pair of ears on each head. Then, count by twos to figure out how many ears are on the page.

_____   _____   _____

_____   _____   _____

_____ ears

Friends

Count by twos to figure out how many people are on the page.

_____   _____   _____

_____   _____   _____

_____   _____   _____

_____ friends

Ballet

Each tu-tu needs two ballet slippers to complete the outfit. Draw the missing ballet slippers. Then, count by twos to figure out how many ballet slippers are on the page.

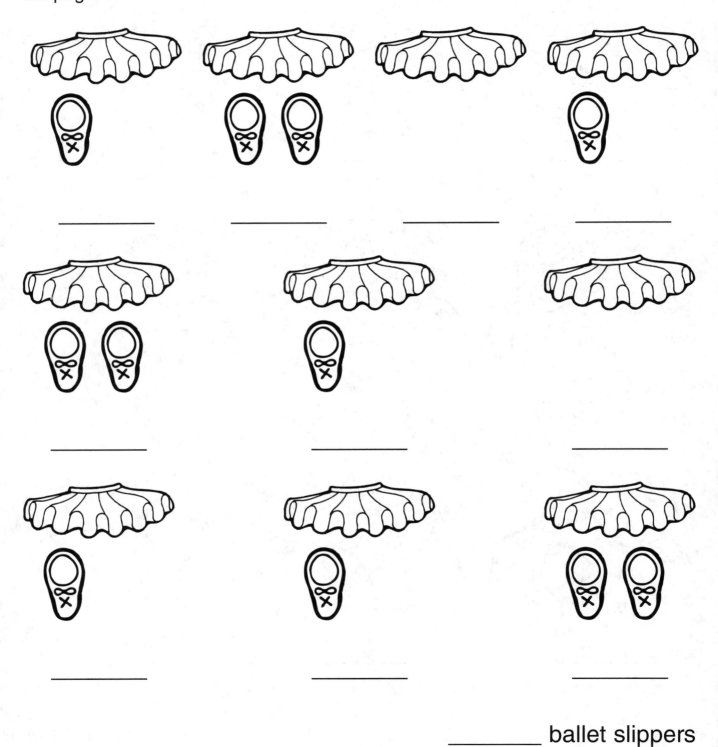

_____ ballet slippers

Barrettes

Draw two barrettes in each girl's hair. Then, count by twos to figure out how many barrettes are in the room.

_____ barrettes

Knee Pads

These football players need knee pads to protect their knees. Draw a set of knee pads on each player. Then, count by twos to figure out how many knee pads are on the page.

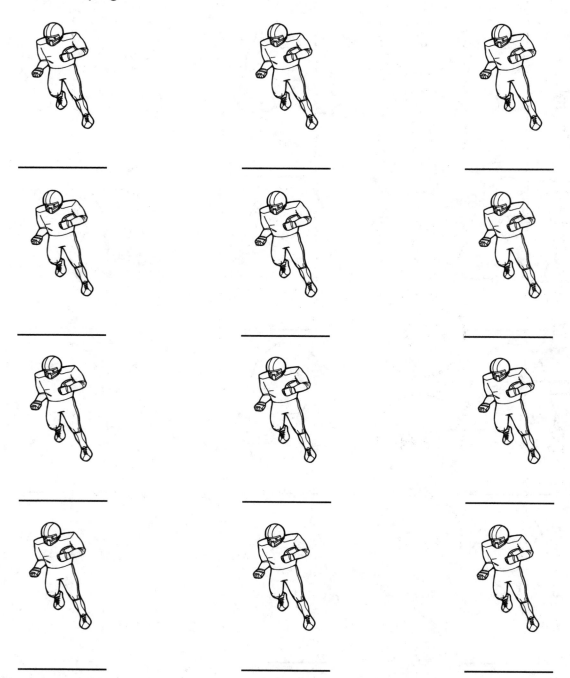

_____ knee pads

Cut It Out

Count by twos to help you complete the patterns below.

1	3	5	
9	11	13	
17	19	21	
25	27	29	
32	34	36	
42	44	46	

Cut out the circles. Then, use them to complete the patterns above.

48   15   31   7   23   38

9   #5981 Start to Finish: Skip Counting

Dalmatian

Finish the number pattern by coloring in the correct answers in the Dalmatian's spots.

1, 3, 5...

Snowflakes

Finish the number pattern by coloring in the correct answers in the snowflakes.

2, 4, 6...

7

8

9

10

11

12

13

14

15

Stickers

There are two stickers in each package. Count by twos to figure out how many stickers this little girl has.

_____ stickers

Caterpillars

Finish the pattern inside each caterpillar.

1   3   5   __   __

2   4   6   __   __

9   11   13   __   __

10   12   14   __   __

15   17   19   __   __

Pond Life

Color in the animal that finishes the number pattern.

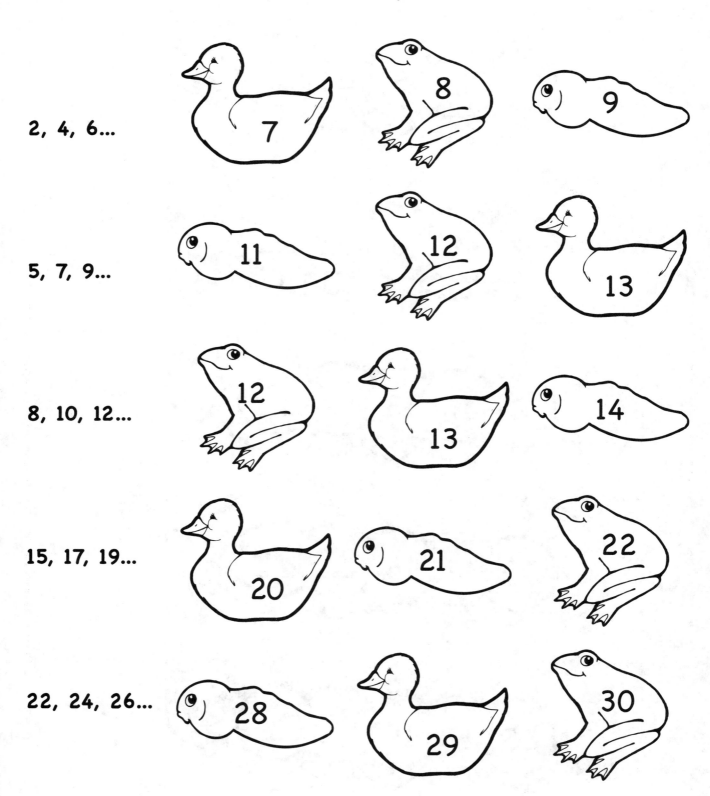

2, 4, 6...   7   8   9

5, 7, 9...   11   12   13

8, 10, 12...   12   13   14

15, 17, 19...   20   21   22

22, 24, 26...   28   29   30

Sweet Tweets

This house is filled with birds! Count by twos to figure out how many birds live in this house!

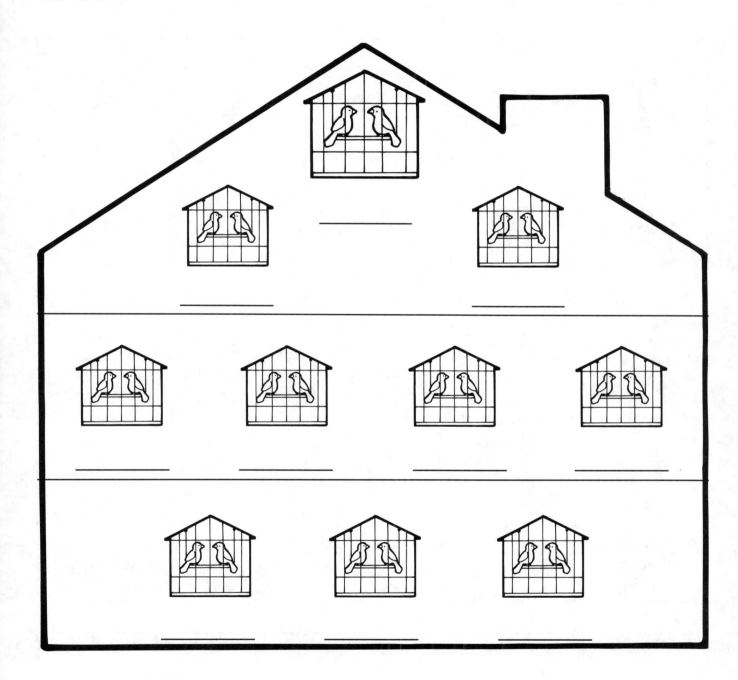

How many birds live in this house? _____

Checkerboard

Start by coloring in the square with the number two. Then, continue counting by twos to figure out which other squares to color.

1	2	3	4	5
6	7	8	9	10
11	12	13	14	15
16	17	18	19	20
21	22	23	24	25
26	27	28	29	30

Pebble Pyramid

Start by coloring in the pebbles 1, 3 and 5. Then, continue counting by twos to figure out which other pebbles to color.

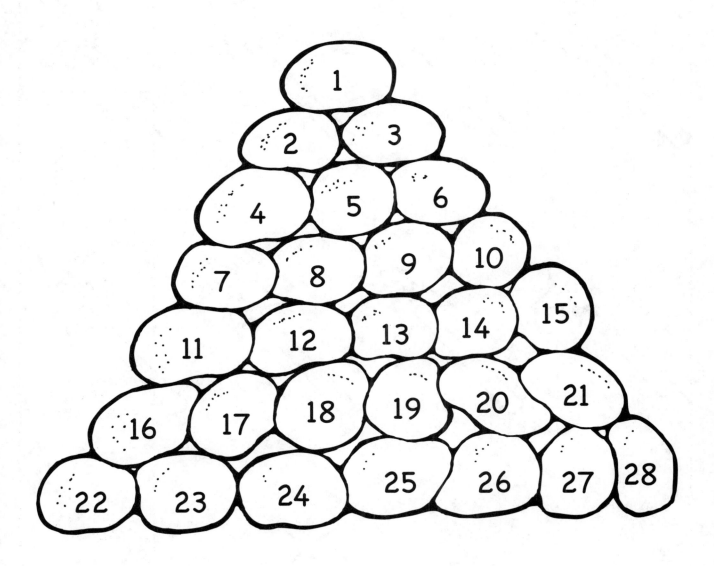

Princess Wands

Start by coloring in the wand with the number five. Then, continue counting by twos to figure out which other wands to color.

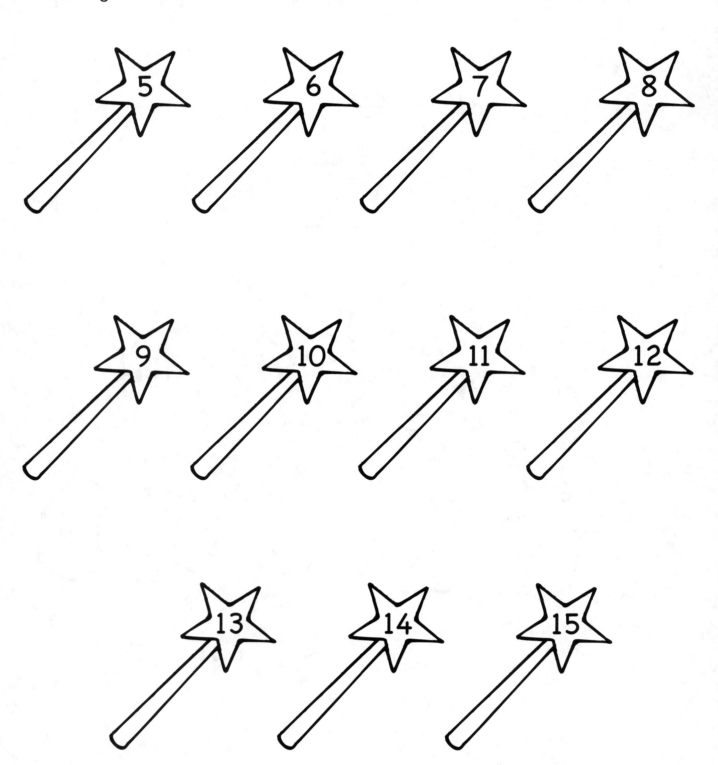

Wizard Caps

Start by coloring in the cap with the number six. Then, continue counting by twos to figure out which other caps to color.

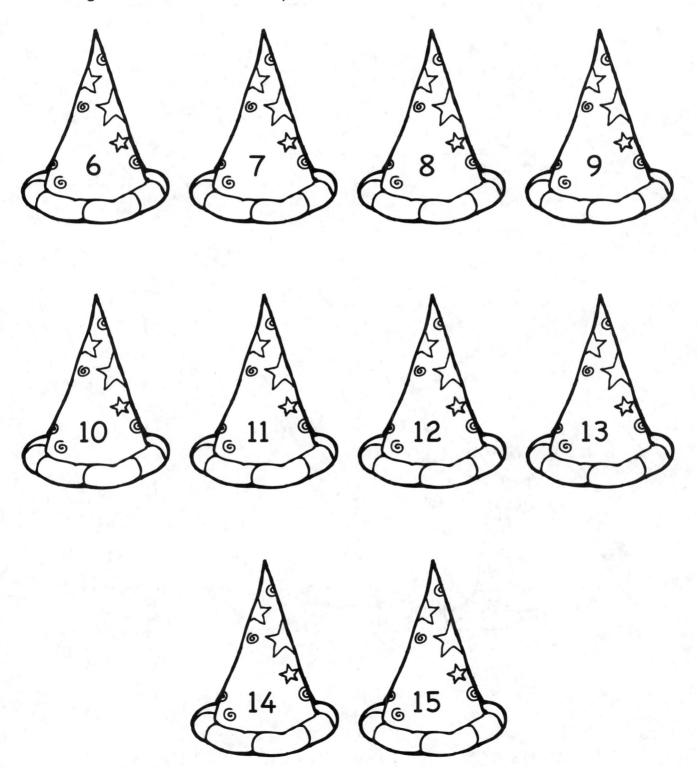

Trees of Threes

Count by threes to figure out how many trees are growing around the building.

How many trees are growing around the building? _____

Magic Beans

Count by threes to figure out how many magic beans are on the page!

How many magic beans are there? _____

Butterflies

Count by threes to figure out how many butterflies live in the garden.

_____ butterflies

$3 Store

Every item in the store costs three dollars. How much will you have to pay for all your items?

_____

_____

_____

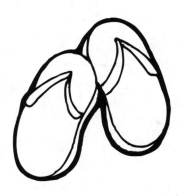

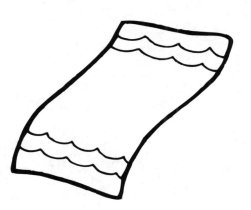

_____

_____

_____

How much do all the items cost? _____

Triceratops

Count by threes to figure out how many horns are on the page.

_____   _____   _____

_____   _____   _____

_____   _____

How many horns are on the page? _____

Pumpkin Pie

Finish the number pattern by coloring in the correct answers in the pumpkin pies.

3, 6, 9. . .

10   11   12

13   14   15

16   17   18

19   20

Polka Dots

Finish the number pattern by coloring in the correct answers in the polka dots.

3, 6, 9. . .

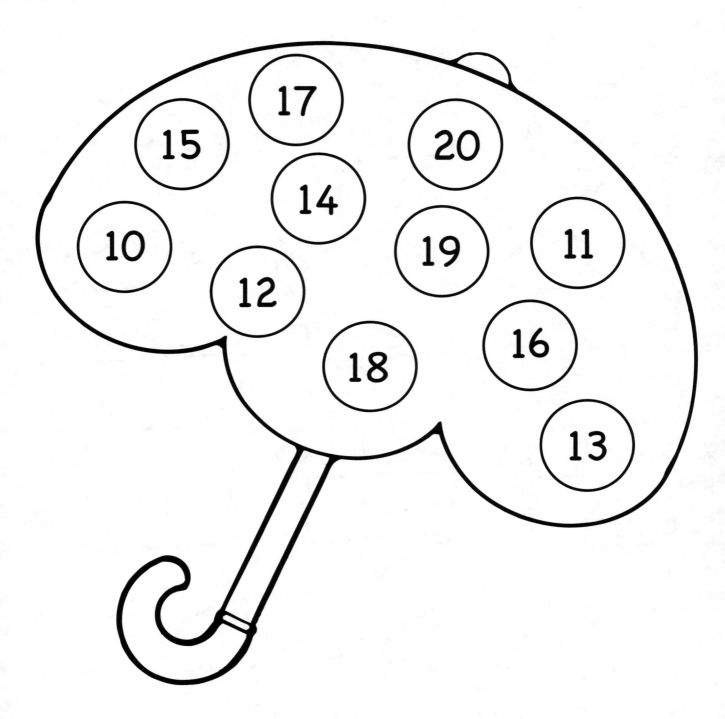

Cat Tails

Finish the number pattern by coloring in the correct answers on the cats' tails.

3, 6, 9. . .

Macaroni

Finish the number pattern by coloring in the correct answers in the macaroni noodles.

3, 6, 9. . . .

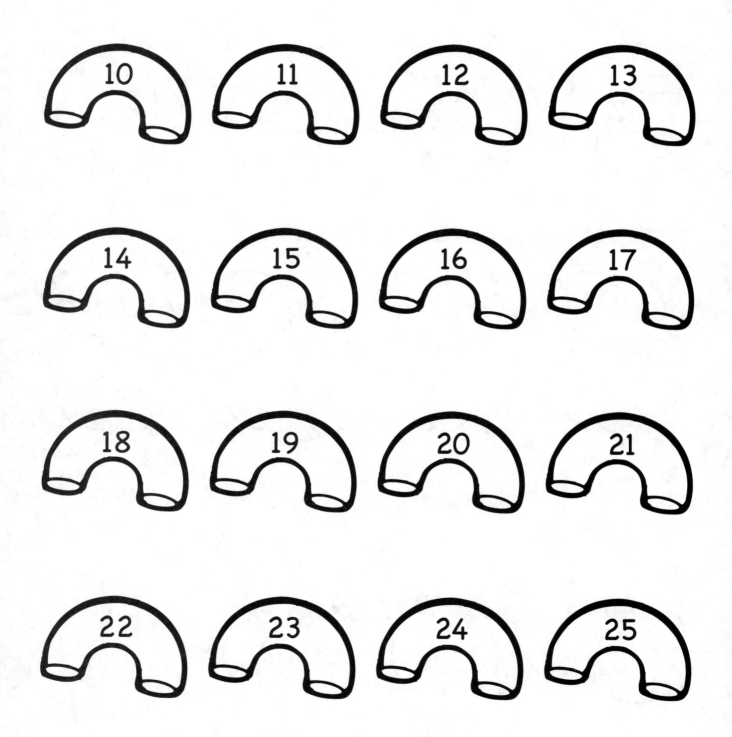

10   11   12   13

14   15   16   17

18   19   20   21

22   23   24   25

Paint Cans

Finish the number pattern by coloring in the paint cans that have the correct numbers on them.

9, 12, 15. . .

16   17   18   19

20   21   22   23

24   25   26   27

28   29   30   31

Seed Packets

There are three seeds in each seed packet. Count by threes to figure out how many flowers will grow once the seeds are planted.

_____ seeds

Fairy Wings

Count by fours to figure out how many wings are on the page.

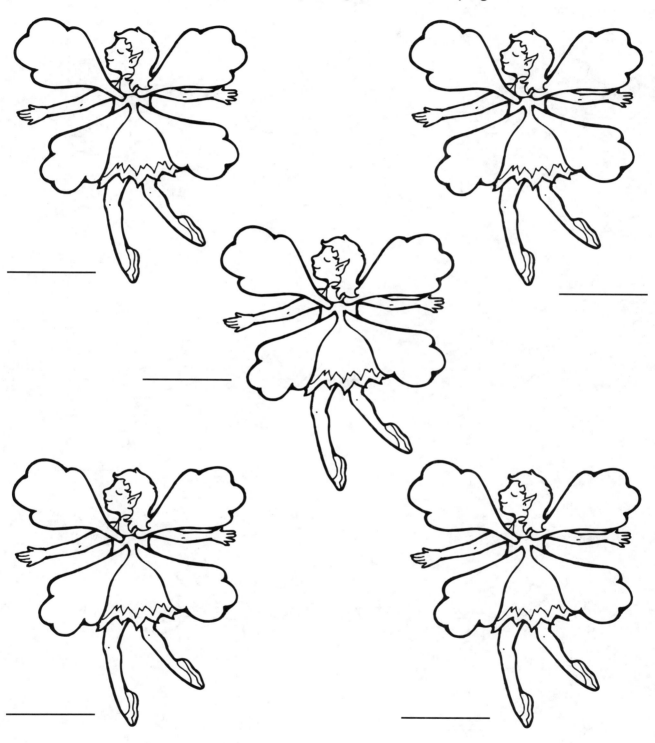

_____

_____

_____

_____

_____

_____ fairy wings

Soar with Four

These birds fly together in fours. Count by fours to figure out how many birds are flying south for the winter.

_____   _____   _____

_____   _____

_____   _____

_____ birds

Four Cores

There are four seeds inside of each apple. Count by fours to figure out how many apple seeds are on the plate.

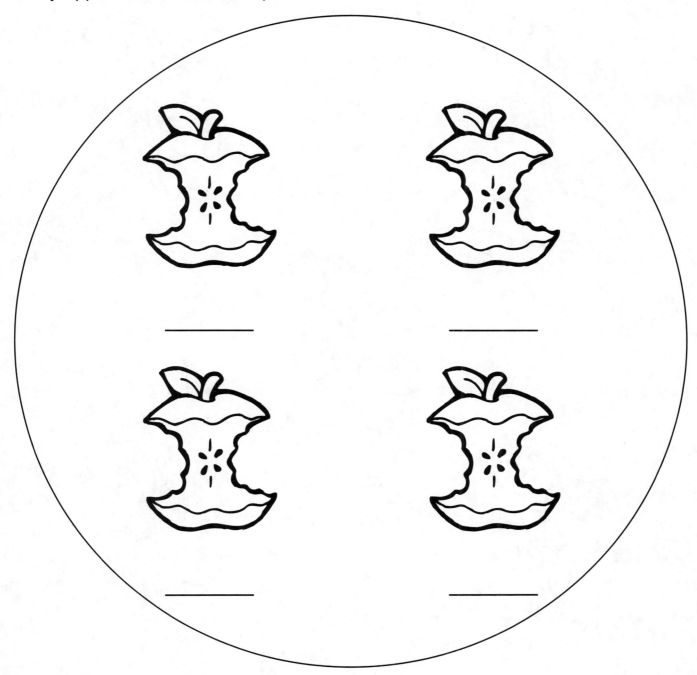

How many apple seeds are on the plate? _____

Tomato Plants

Count by fours to figure out how many tomatoes are growing in the garden.

_____

_____

_____

_____

_____

_____ tomatoes

Four Figs

There are four figs growing on each branch of the fig tree. Count by fours to figure out how many figs are growing.

_____

_____

_____

_____

_____

_____

_____ figs

Number Drums

Finish the number pattern by coloring in the drums with the correct answers in them.

4, 8, 12. . .

13

14

15

16

17

18

19

20

36

Clowning Around

Count by fours to figure out how many clowns are performing at the show.

_____   _____

_____   _____   _____

_____   _____

How many clowns are performing at the show? _____

               #5981 Start to Finish: Skip Counting

Cars

Finish the number pattern by coloring in the cars with the correct answers on them.

4, 8, 12. . .

Beads

Count by fives to figure out how many beads are on the necklace.

How many beads are on the necklace? _____

Buttons

There are five buttons on each shirt. Count by fives to figure out how many buttons are on the page.

_____   _____   _____

_____   _____   _____

_____   _____   _____

_____ buttons

Stripes

Count by fives to figure out how many stripes are painted on the eggs.

_____   _____   _____

_____   _____   _____

_____   _____   _____

_____   _____

_____ stripes

Frog Warts

Draw five warts on each frog. Then, count by fives to figure out how many warts you drew.

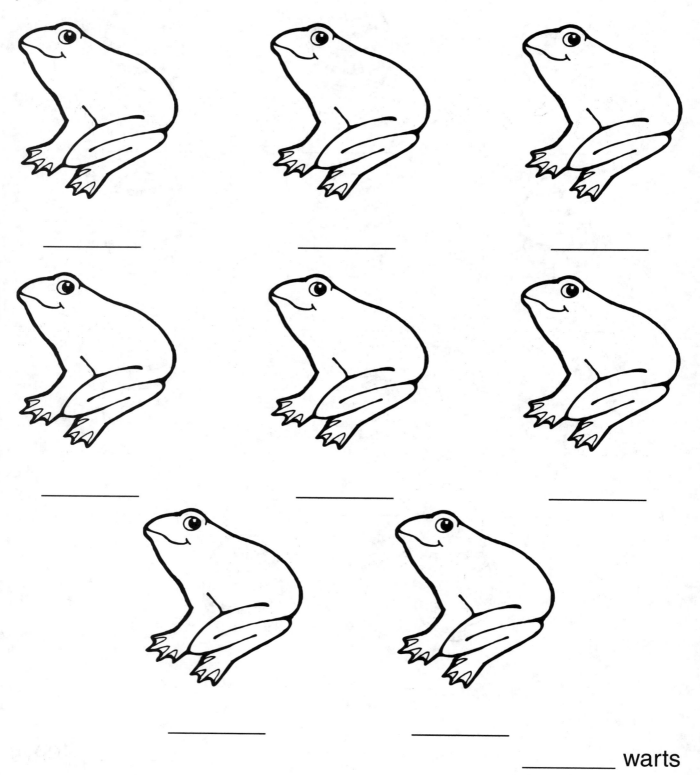

_____   _____   _____

_____   _____   _____

_____   _____

_____ warts

Keys

Count by fives to see how many keys are hanging on the key rings. There are five keys on each ring.

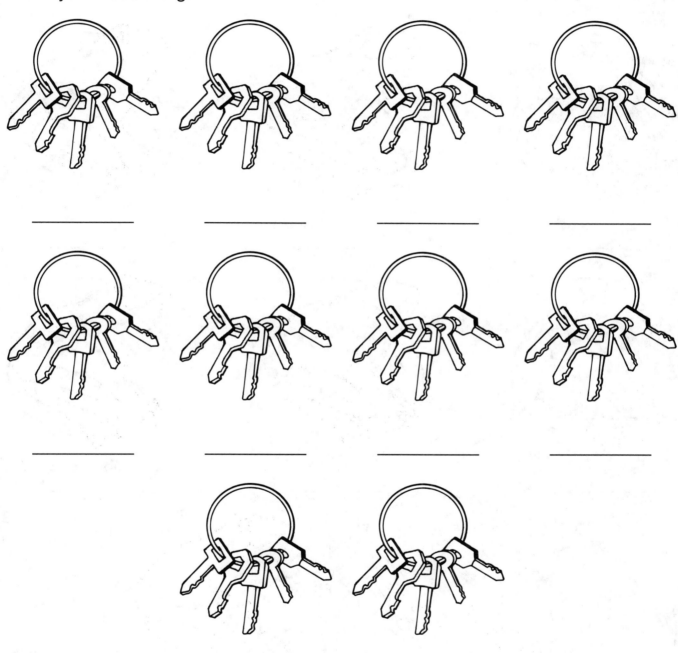

_____ keys

Veggies

There are five vegetables in each bag. Count by fives to see how many vegetables there are.

_____   _____   _____

_____   _____   _____

_____   _____   _____ vegetables

Fingers

Each hand has five fingers. Count by fives to figure out how many fingers are on the page.

_____ _____ _____

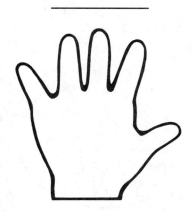  

_____ _____ _____

_____ _____   _____ fingers

Oatmeal

Draw five raisins in each bowl of oatmeal. Then, count by fives to figure out how many raisins you drew.

_____

_____

_____

_____

_____ raisins

Hot Dogs

There are six hot dogs in each package. Count by sixes to figure out how many hot dogs there are.

_____

_____

_____

_____

_____ hot dogs

Straws

Draw six straws in each cup. Then, count by sixes to figure out how many straws you drew.

_____

_____

_____

_____

_____ straws

Special Sacks

Draw seven special items in each of these sacks. Then, count by sevens to see how many items you drew.

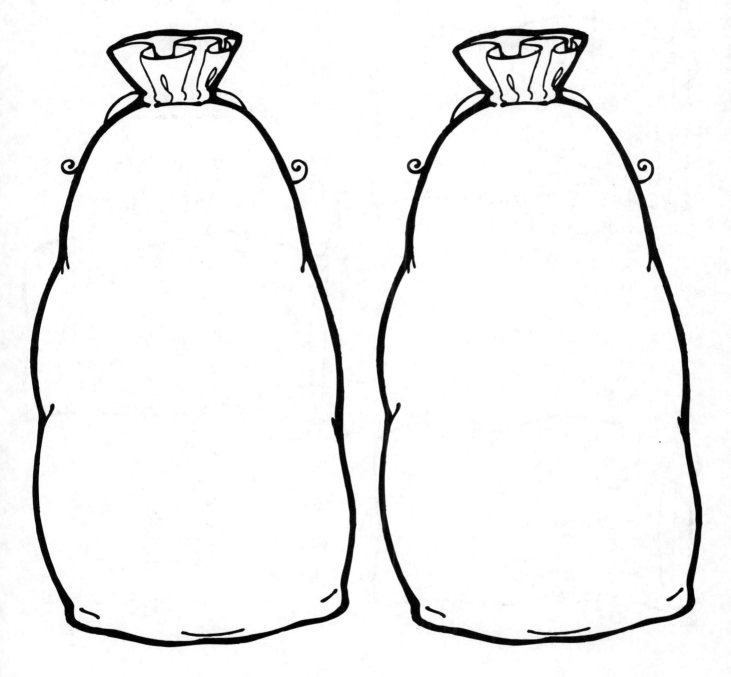

How many items did you draw? _____

Flags

Draw seven stars on each flag. Then, count by sevens to figure out how many stars you drew.

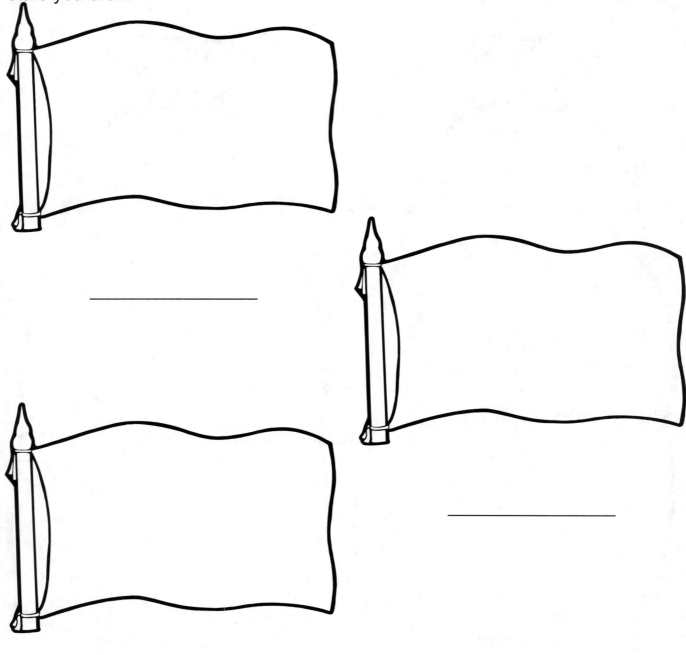

_____

_____

_____

_____ stars

Hats

Draw eight hearts on each of the hats. Then count by eights to figure out how many hearts you drew.

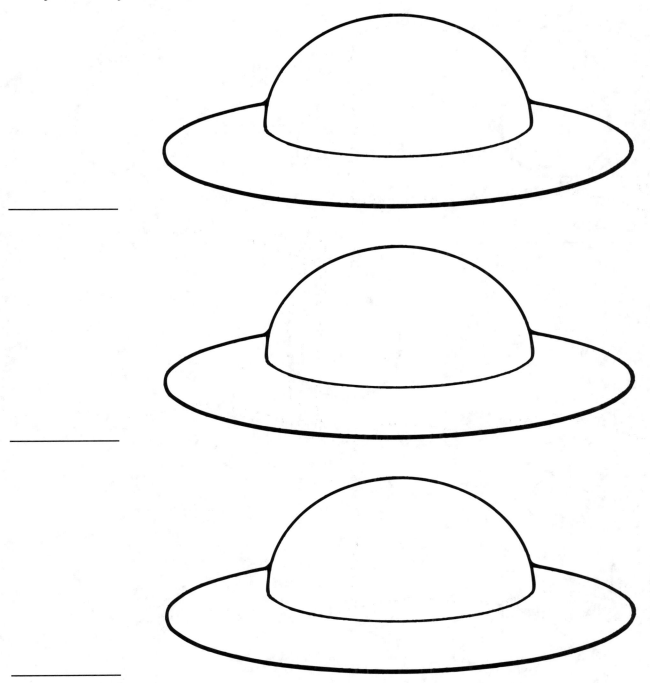

_____

_____

_____

_____ items

Spiders

Spiders have eight legs. Draw eight legs on each of the spiders. Then, count by eights to figure out how many legs you drew.

_____

_____

_____

_____

_____

_____ legs

Roller Skate Wheels

Each pair of roller skates has eight wheels. Count by eights to figure out how many wheels there are altogether.

_____   _____

_____

_____   _____

_____   _____

_____

_____ wheels

Baseball Bats

Each baseball team has nine bats. Count by nines to figure out how many bats there are altogether.

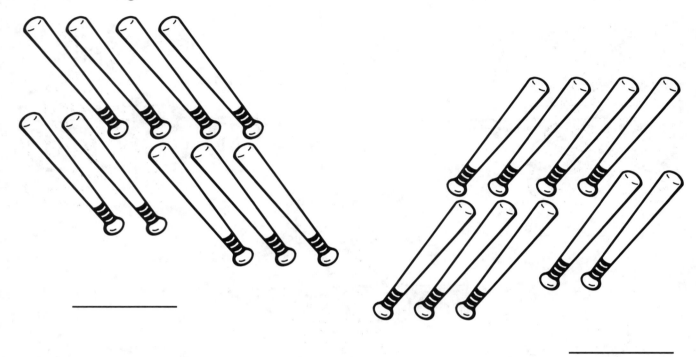

_____

_____

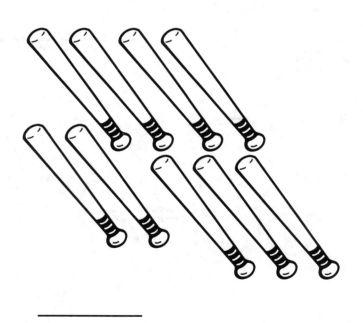

_____

_____ bats

Nine Nuts

There are nine nuts in each bag. Count by nines to figure out how many nuts there are.

_____

_____

_____

_____

_____

_____ nuts

Nine Diners

Nine people will be eating this meal. Count by nines to figure out how many items of food are on the table.

_____

_____

_____

_____

How many items of food were prepared for these diners? _____

Kangaroos

Cut out the kangaroos. Put them in order to complete the number pattern.

10, 20, 30. . .

Washcloths

On each clothesline, there are ten washcloths. Count by tens to figure out how many washcloths there are.

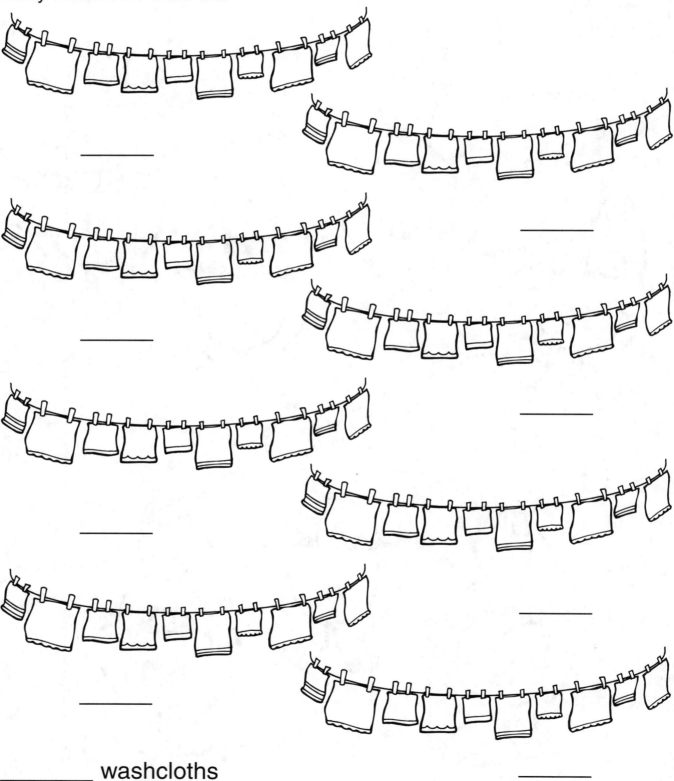

_____ washcloths

Sticky Notes

Cut out the sticky notes. Then, put them in order to complete the number pattern.

11, 21, 31. . .

51

71

61

41

91

81

Numbers on Letters

Figure out the number in order to complete the address labels on the letters.

33 Mathematics Way

43 Mathematics Way

_____ Mathematics Way

_____ Mathematics Way

_____ Mathematics Way

_____ Mathematics Way

Toes

Each pair of feet has 10 toes. Count by tens to figure out how many toes there are altogether.

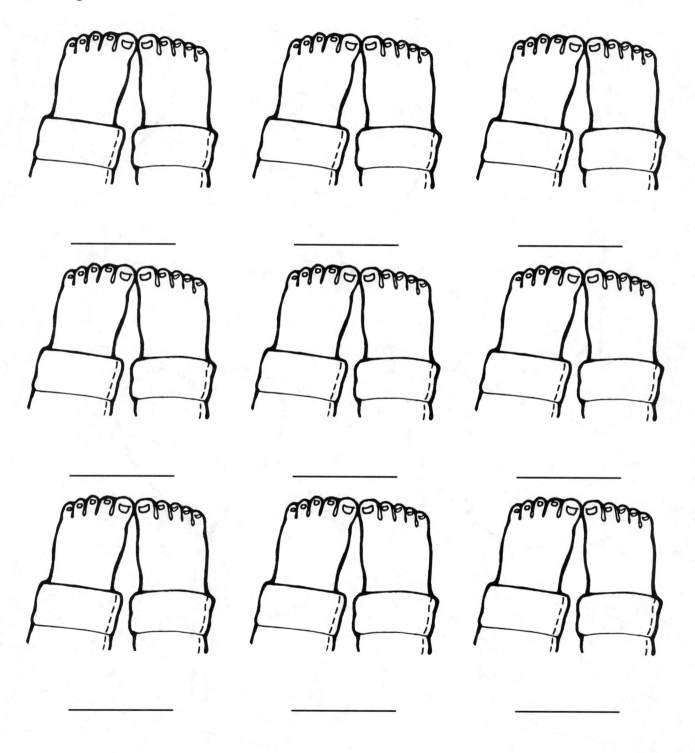

_____   _____   _____

_____   _____   _____

_____   _____   _____

_____ toes

Lollipops

Draw 10 polka dots on each lollipop. Then count by tens to figure out how many dots you drew.

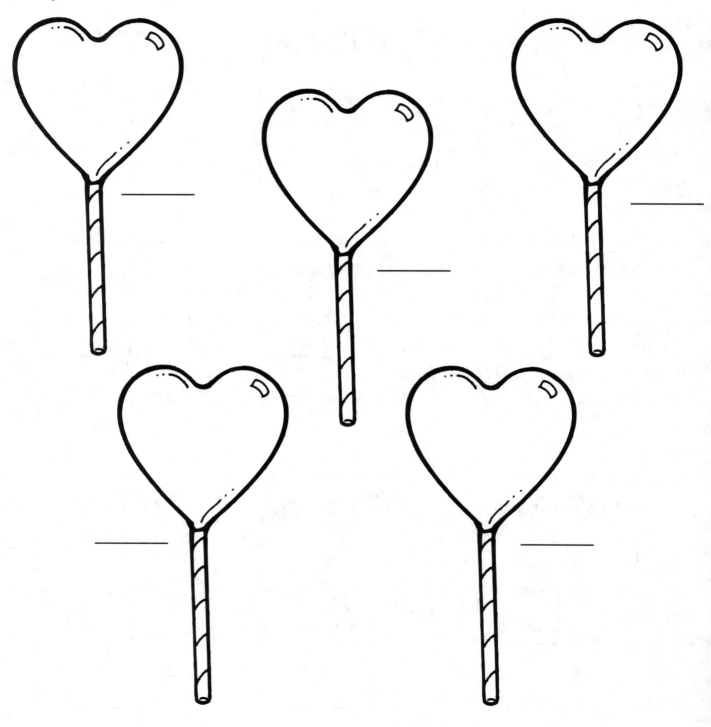

_____ polka dots

Answer Key

Page 4: 12 ears

Page 5: 18 friends

Page 6: 20 ballet slippers

Page 7: 24 barrettes

Page 8: 24 knee pads

Page 9: 7; 15; 23; 31; 38; 48

Page 10: 7, 9, 11, 13, 15

Page 11: 8, 10, 12, 14

Page 12: 24 stickers

Page 13: 7, 9; 8, 10; 15, 17; 16, 18; 21, 23

Page 14: 8; 11; 14; 21; 28

Page 15: 20 birds

Page 16: Colored squares: 2, 4, 6, 8, 10, 12, 14, 16, 18, 20, 22, 24, 26, 28, 30

Page 17: Colored pebbles: 1, 3, 5, 7, 9, 11, 13, 15, 17, 19, 21, 23, 25, 27

Page 18: Colored wands: 5, 7, 9, 11, 13, 15

Page 19: Colored caps: 6, 8, 10, 12, 14

Page 20: 9 trees

Page 21: 21 beans

Page 22: 21 butterflies

Page 23: $18.00

Page 24: 24 horns

Page 25: Colored pies: 12, 15, 18

Page 26: Colored polka dots: 12, 15, 18

Page 27: Colored cats: 12, 15, 18

Page 28: Colored macaroni: 12, 15, 18, 21, 24

Page 29: Colored paint cans: 18, 21, 24, 27, 30

Page 30: 36 seeds

Page 31: 20 fairy wings

Answer Key (cont.)

Page 32: 28 birds

Page 33: 16 apple seeds

Page 34: 20 tomatoes

Page 35: 24 figs

Page 36: Colored drums: 16, 20

Page 37: 28 clowns

Page 38: Colored cars: 16, 20, 24, 28

Page 39: 25 beads

Page 40: 45 buttons

Page 41: 55 stripes

Page 42: 40 warts

Page 43: 50 keys

Page 44: 40 vegetables

Page 45: 40 fingers

Page 46: 25 raisins

Page 47: 24 hot dogs

Page 48: 24 straws

Page 49: 14 items

Page 50: 21 stars

Page 51: 24 hearts

Page 52: 40 spider legs

Page 53: 48 wheels

Page 54: 27 bats

Page 55: 45 nuts

Page 56: 36 items of food

Page 57: Kangaroo pattern: 10, 20, 30, 40, 50, 60, 70, 80, 90, 100

Page 58: 80 washcloths

Page 59: Sticky note pattern: 11, 21, 31, 41, 51, 61, 71, 81, 91

Page 60: 53, 63, 73, 83

Page 61: 80 toes

Page 62: 50 polka dots